I0690933

A Field Guide to Endangered Wildlife Coloring Book

Richard K. Walton

Illustrations by Gordon Morrison

Roger Tory Peterson, Consulting Editor

*Sponsored by
the National Wildlife Federation
and the National Audubon Society*

Houghton Mifflin Company Boston 1991

Introduction copyright © 1991
by Roger Tory Peterson.
Text copyright © 1991
by Richard K. Walton.
Illustrations copyright © 1991
by Gordon Morrison.

All rights reserved.

For information about permission to
reproduct selections from this book,
write to Permissions, Houghton Mifflin
Company, 2 Park Street, Boston,
Massachusetts 02108.

Printed in the United States of America

DPI 10 9 8 7 6 5 4 3 2 1

Introduction

Looking at wild animals requires a quick eye, one that is trained to see details. Little things such as the shape of a head, the color of a wing, or the length of a tail distinguish an animal from others like it. Most beginning naturalists soon learn to use Field Guides such as *A Field Guide to Birds* or *A Field Guide to Mammals.* These handy, pocket-size books offer short cuts to identification, with clear illustrations complete with arrows pointing to the special features of each animal. Because there are many different types of endangered animals in this coloring book, they are found in many different Field Guides. Though they are in danger, they are luckier than some — many of the animals shown here can be seen only in books about extinct species. We hope that all those that are included in today's Guides will still exist to be identified by tomorrow's budding naturalists.

This coloring book is a Field Guide for those who want to sharpen their powers of observation. By filling in the illustrations during evenings at home, you will condition your memory for the days you spend outdoors identifying animals. You will teach yourself to recognize the vast variety in the subtle colors. And you will read about why an endangered animal's habitat is so important to its survival.

Exploring the outdoors, watching the birds and other animals, can be many things — an art, a science, a game, or a sport — but it always sharpens the senses, especially the eye. If you draw or paint, you transfer the images of your eye and mind onto paper. In the process, you become more aware of the natural world — the real world — and inevitably you become an environmentalist.

Most of you will find colored pencils best suited for coloring this book, but if you are handy with brushes and paints, you may prefer to fill in the outlines with watercolors. Crayons, too, can be used. Don't labor too much over getting the colors exactly right; have fun, but remember the plight of the endangered animals you are getting to know.

Roger Tory Peterson

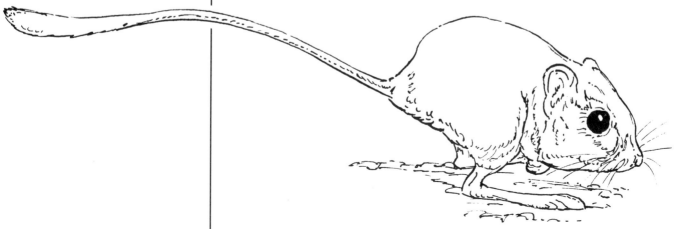

About This Book

There are many different kinds of animals in this coloring book — birds, wolves, sea animals, snakes, and more. They make their homes in many different kinds of places, from mossy evergreen forests to sandy river banks. All these animals have one thing in common: they are endangered species. They are in danger of becoming extinct, or disappearing from the face of the Earth.

Notice that we are not talking about individuals, but about species, or types of animals. For example, the raccoon in your neighborhood may be endangered by traffic or threatened by dogs, but raccoons in general are not in danger of becoming extinct. Extinct animals are lost forever.

There are many reasons why an animal becomes extinct, and we will talk about those reasons throughout the book. Most of the animals shown here, though, are endangered because of humans. When we move into a wild place, we immediately start changing it to suit our needs. We cut down the forests to build our houses and cities. We clear the land to make room for our crops. We dam up the rivers to get our water. We bring with us our dogs, sheep, and cattle. All of these things make it harder for wild animals to live in their homes, or habitats. And if this isn't enough to make them disappear, sometimes we actively hunt and poison them into extinction.

You are probably familiar with the plight of many of the animals in this book, such as the Grizzly Bear, Blue Whale, Bald Eagle, and California Condor. Others, such as the Plymouth Redbelly Turtle, Wyoming Toad, and American Burying Beetle, are less well known but no less deserving of our protection. Some species that have wide ranges, such as the Bald Eagle, are endangered only in some areas. Others, such as the Paiute Trout, have always had small home ranges and so are even more sensitive to damage done to their habitats.

You will notice that many endangered species are concentrated in a relatively few areas of the United States. The coast of California, south Florida, and Hawaii, for example, have more than their share of endangered animals. This is not just a coincidence. The simple fact is that the natural habitats of those areas, including the rivers, grasslands, and forests, have been drastically altered or eliminated to meet the needs of humans. Interestingly, some species actually benefit from manmade changes, but many more are suffering. In south Florida, for instance, Opossums and sea gulls are thriving, while Snail Kites, Florida Panthers, Wood Storks, and Manatees are rapidly disappearing. Of course, other states and regions have their share of endangered species, too. In North America, there are over 500 endangered or threatened species. Another 1,500 plants and animals are candidates for the endangered list. Chances are there are several endangered species in your state.

Florida Panther: Florida Panther, eastern mountain lion, and cougar are different names for the same animal. All of these wild cats were hunted relentlessly by settlers who feared for their livestock, until the cats had disappeared from most parts of the East by the mid-1800s.

This century has brought more threats. The Florida Panther's habitat has disappeared as land has been been cleared and swamps drained. Now panthers face another threat — traffic. Many panthers have been killed by cars. There are now fewer than 50 panthers left in south Florida. Some researchers want to try breeding the panthers in captivity and releasing them. But their habitat is disappearing so quickly, there may be no place for the Florida Panther to go.

This magnificent cat may grow to be 7 feet long, including the tail, and weigh 120 pounds. It is reddish brown on top, gray below, and has tawny flanks. It is often mistakenly called "black panther." **(27)**

27. Florida Panther

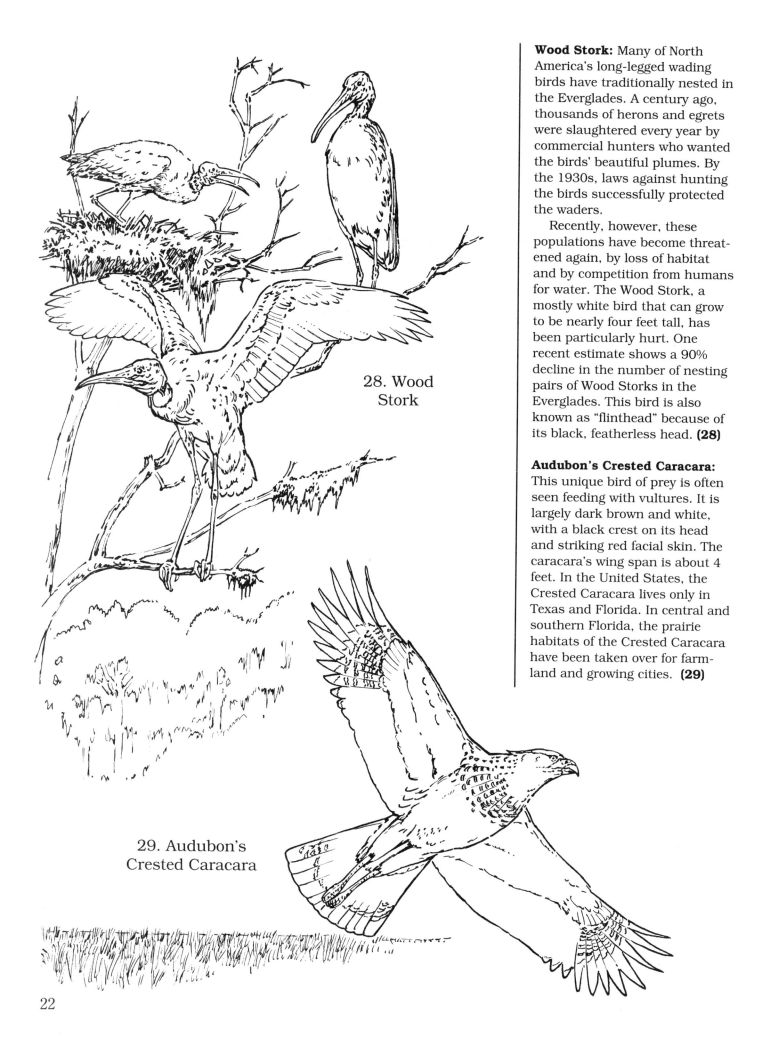

28. Wood Stork

29. Audubon's Crested Caracara

Wood Stork: Many of North America's long-legged wading birds have traditionally nested in the Everglades. A century ago, thousands of herons and egrets were slaughtered every year by commercial hunters who wanted the birds' beautiful plumes. By the 1930s, laws against hunting the birds successfully protected the waders.

Recently, however, these populations have become threatened again, by loss of habitat and by competition from humans for water. The Wood Stork, a mostly white bird that can grow to be nearly four feet tall, has been particularly hurt. One recent estimate shows a 90% decline in the number of nesting pairs of Wood Storks in the Everglades. This bird is also known as "flinthead" because of its black, featherless head. **(28)**

Audubon's Crested Caracara: This unique bird of prey is often seen feeding with vultures. It is largely dark brown and white, with a black crest on its head and striking red facial skin. The caracara's wing span is about 4 feet. In the United States, the Crested Caracara lives only in Texas and Florida. In central and southern Florida, the prairie habitats of the Crested Caracara have been taken over for farmland and growing cities. **(29)**

Brown Pelican: Brown Pelicans are large water birds with a wingspan of 7 feet. They are perhaps best known for their impressive feeding dives, when they plunge head-first into a school of fish. Once common along the East, West, and Gulf coasts, many of the Brown Pelicans were wiped out by DDT-type pesticides in the late 1950s. The Gulf Coast was especially hard hit, and nearly all of the 50,000 pelicans in Louisiana and Texas disappeared. In 1972 a law was passed banning DDT, and the Brown Pelican began to make a comeback. **(30)**

30. Brown Pelican

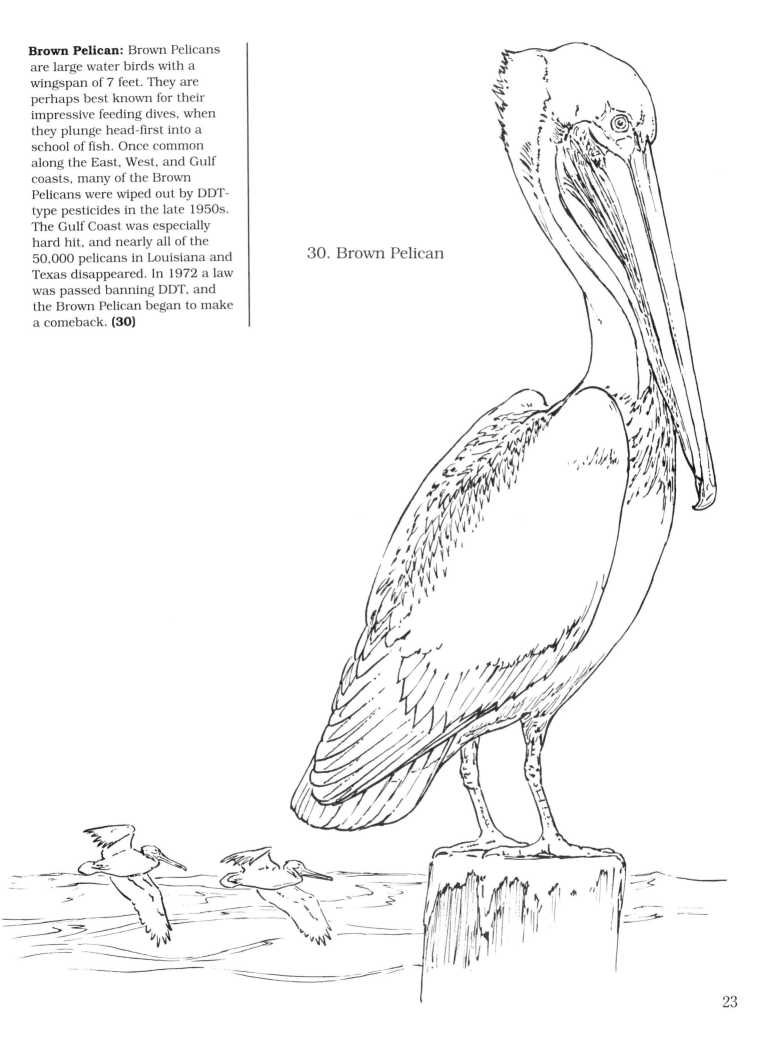

31. Piping
Plover

32. Least Tern

Endangered Birds
Shore Birds

Piping Plover: This small bird makes a shallow nest in the sand along the shore of the ocean or a lake. The plover's pale feathers are the color of dry sand, good camouflage in its sandy habitat. Often the only sign of a nesting pair is a weak, melodious whistle. Unfortunately, this call is seldom heard or heeded by drivers of off-road vehicles, who often plunge through the plover's nesting territories. The big challenge for those trying to save the Piping Plover is educating motorized beach goers that their vehicles may disturb or destroy the plover's nesting efforts. **(31)**

Least Tern: Like the Piping Plover, Least Terns live both on the coast and inland. They nest near large rivers such as the Ohio, the Mississippi, and the Missouri. At least they used to, until man-made dams on the rivers permanently flooded many traditional nesting sites.

Least Terns are only about 9 inches long. They are pale gray and white, and have a yellow bill and yellow feet. **(32)**

Roseate Tern: In North America, most Roseate Terns nest on a few islands along the Massachusetts coast. Nesting birds are usually successful at hatching their eggs. But because the birds are concentrated in such a small area, a single environmental disaster could wipe out the entire species. Recently, Roseate Terns have been dying of unknown causes during the winter, and their numbers are decreasing.

Roseate Terns look much like Least Terns, but they are paler and have a black bill. **(33)**

33. Roseate Tern

34. Golden-cheeked Warbler

35. Black-capped Vireo

Song Birds

Golden-cheeked Warbler: Golden-cheeked Warblers nest only in the hill country of central Texas. Here on the wooded slopes and canyonsides of the Edwards Plateau are their oak and juniper nesting territories. But cities are gradually pushing into the area, and much of this habitat has been destroyed. As a result, the population has declined drastically in the last decades. Perhaps fewer than 2,000 pairs of Golden-cheeked Warblers are left.

Males have a black back and black throat, females have an olive green back. All have bright yellow cheeks. **(34)**

Black-capped Vireo: Another endangered Texas songbird is the Black-capped Vireo. This small (4½ inches) bird has an olive green or gray back, white "spectacles," and red eyes.

The Black-capped Vireo faces many threats, from destruction of its Edwards Plateau habitat to predators and nest parasites such as the Brown-headed Cowbird. The cowbirds often invade the nests of other species when the parent birds are away, laying their own eggs in the nests. Often the hosts raise the young cowbirds as their own, even though they may crowd out the hosts' own babies. House cats, Scrub Jays, and Fire Ants also prey on the vireos. **(35)**

Bachman's Warbler: This is the rarest songbird in North America — that is, if it still exists. Recent reports of Bachman's Warblers are exceedingly scarce, and the few remaining birds may be succumbing to pressures on their prime habitat, southern river-bottom swamps. Bachman's Warbler is olive green on top, yellow below. The males have a black throat. This species is named for John Bachman, who discovered it in 1833 in Charleston, South Carolina. John James Audubon, the great naturalist and bird painter, first described this rare warbler although he himself never saw one. **(36)**

Kirtland's Warbler: Here is another very rare North American bird. This warbler, which has a yellow belly streaked with black, nests in young Jack Pines. This habitat is available only in areas where fires periodically revamp the landscape and allow new growth. At present, such new growth is being encouraged in Huron National Forest, Michigan, by controlled burning. This is the only large nesting area for Kirtland's Warbler.

Like the Black-capped Vireo, this species is threatened by Brown-headed Cowbirds. **(37)**

36. Bachman's Warbler

37. Kirtland's Warbler

38. Mississippi
Sandhill Crane

39. Whooping
Crane

Cranes and Other Birds

Mississippi Sandhill Crane: The Mississippi Sandhill Crane is considered the world's rarest and most endangered crane. Only about 50 of these birds still live in the wild. They do not migrate, but live year-round in the Mississippi Sandhill Crane National Wildlife Refuge, their only home. Some birds have been bred in captivity and added to the wild population.

Sandhill Cranes are tall gray birds with a red bald patch on the crown of their head. **(38)**

Whooping Crane: At over 4 feet tall, Whooping Cranes are the tallest birds in North America. They are white with a red face and have a call that sounds like a bugle. In 1945 there were only 21 Whooping Cranes still alive. Most of these birds belonged to a migratory group that wintered on Texas's Gulf Coast and spent the summer in Canada.

From this dangerous low point, the number of Whooping Cranes has increased to over 200 birds, thanks to strict laws protecting their habitat and successful breeding in captivity. Whooping Cranes are still threatened by careless hunters, pollution, and the possibility of lethal oil spills. **(39)**

Light-footed Clapper Rail:
Clapper Rails, or "marsh hens," are large birds that live in the coastal marshes of southern California. This large rail is about 16 inches long; it is brownish with white belly bands and a cinnamon-colored chest.

The fate of the Light-footed Clapper Rail depends on the preservation and well-being of its habitat. Unfortunately, most of these marshes have been drained and filled for housing. One estimate is that the coastal wetlands are now less than one third their original size. As the coastal marshes are reduced, so are the numbers of rails. By the late 1970s only 300 or so Light-footed Clapper Rails remained in California. **(40)**

Attwater's Prairie Chicken: The Greater Prairie Chicken is a native of tall-grass prairies. The males, with bright yellow neck pouches and dark "horns," take up positions on their booming grounds in spring, where they vie for the attention of the females.

On the plains along the coast of Texas, Attwater's Prairie Chicken, a small race of the Greater Prairie Chicken, struggles to survive in the ever-shrinking patches of native coastal prairie. Several Texas refuges have set aside land for the prairie chickens, but increasing urban needs continue to threaten the bird. **(41)**

40. Light-footed Clapper Rail

41. Attwater's Prairie Chicken

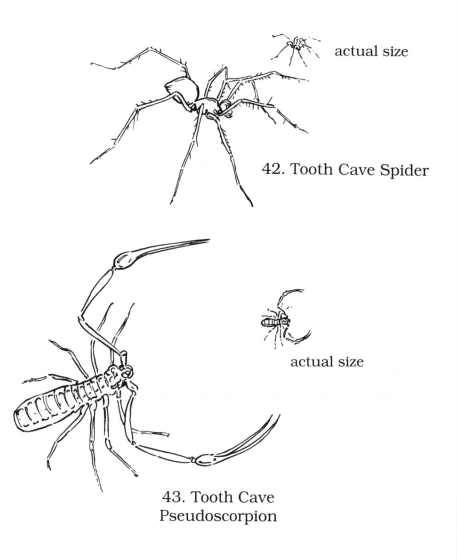

actual size

42. Tooth Cave Spider

43. Tooth Cave
Pseudoscorpion

actual size

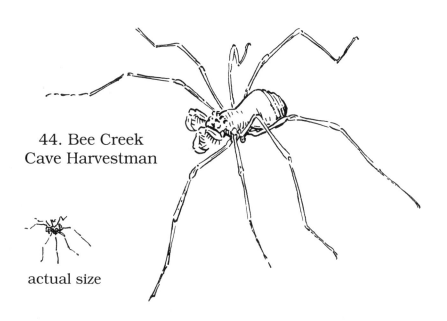

44. Bee Creek
Cave Harvestman

actual size

Arachnids

Spiders are the best known arachnids. Other animals in this class of invertebrates (animals without backbones) include scorpions, harvestmen, mites, and ticks. Arachnids have eight legs, while insects have six.

The three endangered arachnids shown here all live in limestone caves of the Edwards Plateau in central Texas. Development has increased here in the last several decades, especially around cities such as Austin and San Antonio. (See also the Golden-cheeked Warbler and Black-capped Vireo on page 26, two more residents of the endangered Edwards Plateau.)

There are half a dozen endangered species living in Tooth Cave in the Edwards Plateau, including three arachnids. New roads and suburban development have significantly damaged the habitat of the Tooth Cave system.

Tooth Cave Spider: This spider is pale pink, a typical color for animals that spend their entire lives in the dark. It is only a tenth of an inch long. **(42)**

Tooth Cave Pseudoscorpion: Like many cave-dwellers, this arachnid has no eyes. Pseudoscorpions look like miniature scorpions, but they don't have a stinger. **(43)**

Bee Creek Cave Harvestman: Here is a tiny (⅛ inch) relative of the daddy long legs. It is yellowish brown and has very long, slender legs. **(44)**

Herps

Although there are clear differences between amphibians and reptiles, the two groups are often lumped together as "herps," a short form of the word *herpetology*, which is the study of reptiles and amphibians. The group includes frogs, toads, and salamanders (the amphibians) as well as snakes, turtles, lizards, and crocodilians (the reptiles).

Reptiles

Reptiles have scaly skin that keeps them from drying out. This makes reptiles well adapted to life on land. All reptiles lay their eggs or give birth on land.

New Mexico Ridgenose Rattlesnake: This reddish brown snake with white crossbars can grow to be 2 feet long. A resident of the Animas Mountains in New Mexico, this rattlesnake has a ridge on its upper snout. Populations of this snake have always been small, and snake collectors are its biggest threat. **(45)**

Atlantic Salt Marsh Snake: Close relatives of the water snakes that live in fresh water; salt marsh snakes live in brackish or salt water. The Atlantic Salt Marsh Snake grows to 2½ feet. It is tan with straw-colored markings, stripes on the front part of its body and splotches near the tail. This is one of many threatened species in Florida. Destruction of tidal marshes and mangrove swamps has reduced its habitat significantly. **(46)**

Puerto Rican Boa: This large snake is relatively widespread in Puerto Rico and may grow to be 7 feet long. It is brown with many darker splotches on top. This boa's diet includes birds, rodents, and bats. Welcome reforestation in Puerto Rico has made it possible for this boa to expand its habitat. **(47)**

45. New Mexico Ridgenose Rattlesnake

46. Atlantic Salt Marsh Snake

47. Puerto Rican Boa

48. San Francisco Garter Snake

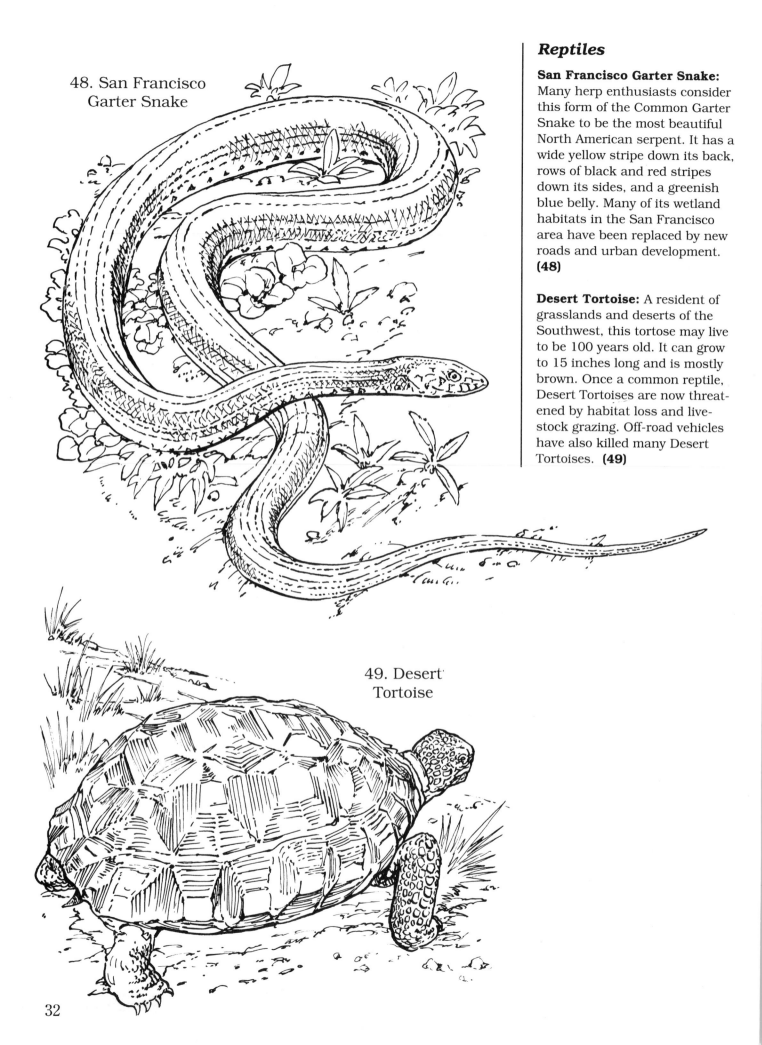

49. Desert Tortoise

Reptiles

San Francisco Garter Snake: Many herp enthusiasts consider this form of the Common Garter Snake to be the most beautiful North American serpent. It has a wide yellow stripe down its back, rows of black and red stripes down its sides, and a greenish blue belly. Many of its wetland habitats in the San Francisco area have been replaced by new roads and urban development. **(48)**

Desert Tortoise: A resident of grasslands and deserts of the Southwest, this tortose may live to be 100 years old. It can grow to 15 inches long and is mostly brown. Once a common reptile, Desert Tortoises are now threatened by habitat loss and live-stock grazing. Off-road vehicles have also killed many Desert Tortoises. **(49)**

Plymouth Redbelly Turtle: This colorful turtle has a dark upper shell with reddish stripes; the lower shell is pinkish. A resident of sandy-shored ponds in Plymouth County, Massachusetts, it is threatened by development and eaten by fish and mammals. Efforts to save this turtle include protection around the ponds and captive breeding programs. **(50)**

Coachella Valley Fringe-toed Lizard: This desert lizard occurs only in the Coachella Valley in southern California. Its pale color with a black speckled pattern on top helps it hide in the sand. Its "fringed toes" have a row of flattened scales that help the reptile move through and burrow into the sand with astonishing speed. When running at top speed, it often runs on its hind legs. Unfortunately, the fringe-toed lizard has had to compete with a construction boom that has taken most of its home territory. Land is now being purchased to establish the Coachella Valley Preserve as a sanctuary for these lizards. **(51)**

50. Plymouth Redbelly Turtle

female

male

51. Coachella Valley Fringe-toed Lizard

33

52. Loggerhead

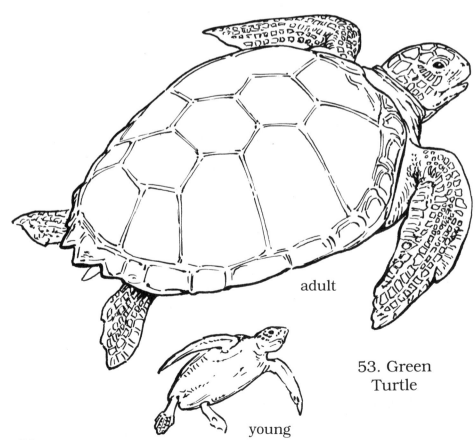

adult

young

53. Green Turtle

Sea Turtles

Sea turtles spend nearly all of their lives in the open ocean. Their flipperlike legs allow them to move efficiently in their watery environment. Once a year, however, they return to sandy shores to lay their eggs, with many species returning to the same beach year after year. Because they lay their eggs in such a predictable way and are defenseless on land, many sea turtle populations have been nearly wiped out. Egg poachers, tortoiseshell and meat hunters, and even aphrodisiac seekers all kill hundreds of sea turtles every year.

Another important cause of sea turtle death is shrimp nets. Commercial shrimp fishers use nets that trap and drown over 10,000 sea turtles each year. Many turtles could be saved if the shrimpers would use devices that keep turtles out of the nets, and in fact there are laws requiring their use. Still, some shrimpers don't comply.

Loggerhead: The Loggerhead can weigh as much as a quarter ton. Its upper shell is reddish brown, and its head is yellowish or tan. When baby Loggerheads emerge from their nests, they find the sea by heading for a bright area such as would be caused by moonlight on the water. In areas where there is beachfront development, Loggerheads often mistakenly aim for beachfront lights instead of crawling to the ocean. Local laws limiting lighting have helped more hatchlings find the sea. **(52)**

Green Turtle: This species is a popular source of meat as well as the main ingredient of turtle soup. Many animals that escape the meat hunters are caught in shrimp nets and die. Brown in color (its name comes from the green color of its fat), the Green Turtle can weigh more than 650 pounds. **(53)**

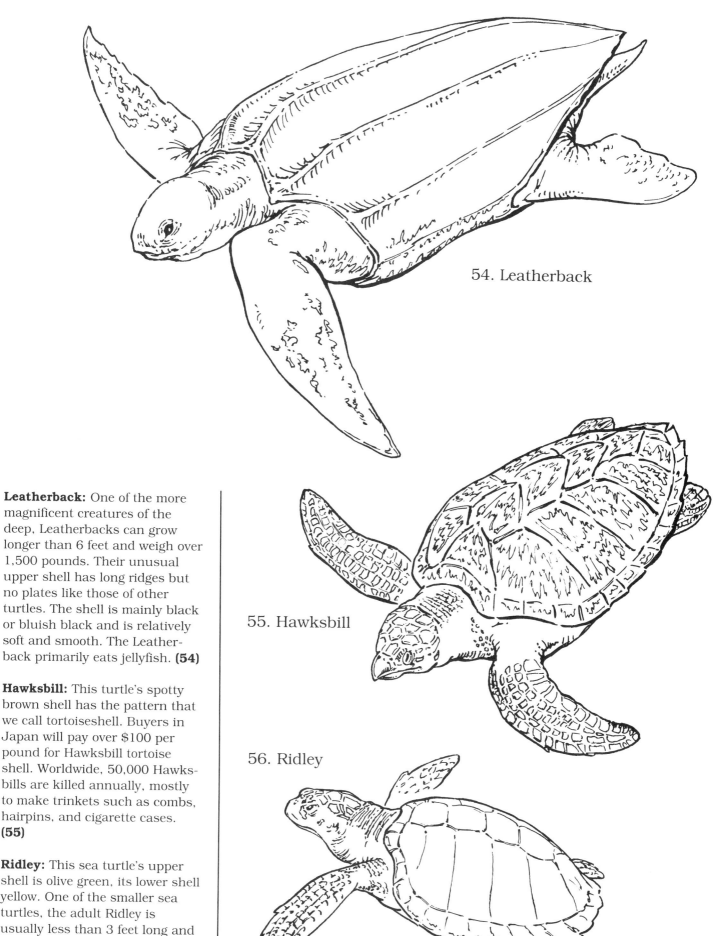

54. Leatherback

Leatherback: One of the more magnificent creatures of the deep, Leatherbacks can grow longer than 6 feet and weigh over 1,500 pounds. Their unusual upper shell has long ridges but no plates like those of other turtles. The shell is mainly black or bluish black and is relatively soft and smooth. The Leatherback primarily eats jellyfish. **(54)**

Hawksbill: This turtle's spotty brown shell has the pattern that we call tortoiseshell. Buyers in Japan will pay over $100 per pound for Hawksbill tortoise shell. Worldwide, 50,000 Hawksbills are killed annually, mostly to make trinkets such as combs, hairpins, and cigarette cases. **(55)**

Ridley: This sea turtle's upper shell is olive green, its lower shell yellow. One of the smaller sea turtles, the adult Ridley is usually less than 3 feet long and weighs about 100 pounds. **(56)**

55. Hawksbill

56. Ridley

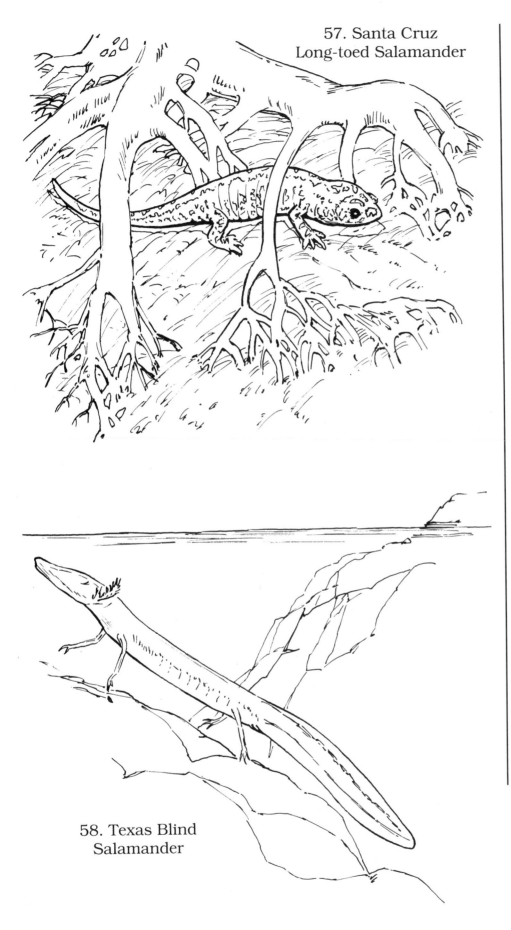

57. Santa Cruz
Long-toed Salamander

58. Texas Blind
Salamander

Amphibians

Amphibians generally have smooth skin through which they take in oxygen. Their skin needs to stay moist so that their "breathing" is efficient. This means that amphibians are largely limited to damp or watery habitats.

All over the world, the numbers of amphibians have been decreasing in recent years. While some scientists feel the amphibian die-off is exaggerated, others believe that something very real is killing many amphibians. Acid rain and other kinds of pollution are suspected causes; so are drought, competition from people, and pesticides.

Santa Cruz Long-toed Salamander:
This salamander is black with yellow-orange markings along its back. It lives only in a few places in Santa Cruz County, California, including Valencia Lagoon and Ellicott Pond. Trailer park development, highway construction, and herp collectors have all threatened the Santa Cruz Long-toed Salamander. **(57)**

Texas Blind Salamander: This ghostly salamander is mostly white, with skin so thin you can almost see its insides. Its only color is a pinkish tinge on its gills and mustard shading on its tail. The Texas Blind Salamander lives in lifelong darkness in the waters of caves in San Marcos, Texas. As human needs for water increase, the underground waterways that feed the caves are drained, making survival harder for the salamanders. **(58)**

Houston Toad: The rare Houston Toad is a relative of the common American Toad. Toads in general are different from many other amphibians in that they have dry skin and spend most of their life on land. They do, however, return to ponds to mate, and it is there that one can hear the high-pitched trills of the males. As the city of Houston, Texas, has grown, much of the its loblolly pine habitat, the home of the Houston Toad, has been destroyed. **(59)**

Wyoming Toad: The Wyoming Toad is tan, with many dark markings and warts. It lives in the wetlands near the Laramie River in Wyoming, and spends more time in the water than most toads. Although the exact causes are not clear, threats to the Wyoming Toad's existence probably include use of herbicides and pesticides. **(60)**

59. Houston Toad

60. Wyoming Toad

37

61. American Bison

62. Grizzly Bear

Endangered Mammals

American Bison (Buffalo):
American Bison weigh up to 2,000 pounds and stand 6 feet tall at the shoulder. There were once 75 million of these huge animals in North America. But in the 1800s, the bison were nearly exterminated by hunters. "Buffalo Bill" Cody, who was hired by the railroad companies to provide food for the workers, shot 4,280 bison in 18 months. Some tourists even made a game out of killing bison, shooting them from the windows of trains. Millions more were slaughtered so that their bones could be made into charcoal. By the end of the 1800s, fewer than 600 animals survived.

A program to save the bison was set up in the nick of time, and herds of bison now roam in several of the West's national parks. **(61)**

Grizzly Bear: The Grizzly weighs up to 850 pounds and may reach 7 feet in length. It has a dished face and a hump over its shoulders. The bears' white-tipped (grizzled) fur ranges in color from golden yellow to black. They eat meat, fruit, and grubs, and they gorge themselves on salmon during the fish's spawning runs.

The Grizzly's size, strength, speed, and apparent lack of fear of humans inspires emotions of fear, awe, and even respect. Historically, Grizzlys have been killed or driven out of areas that humans use. This magnificent animal still roams free in Alaska and northwestern Canada, but in the lower 48 states it is mainly restricted to large wilderness areas such as Glacier National Park. **(62)**

Woodland Caribou: Bigger than a deer but smaller than an elk, the chocolate brown Woodland Caribou weighs up to 600 pounds. The male's antlers have an impressive spread of as much as 5 feet. The Woodland Caribou lives in small family groups and migrates mostly up and down mountains, unlike the Barren Ground Caribou of far northern North America, which is famous for its massive herds and long-distance migrations.

Woodland Caribou once ranged across the United States from New England to the state of Washington. They still range over most of Canada, but many of their homeland forests in the U.S. were cut down. Only a few small herds remain in northern Washington, Idaho, and Montana. **(63)**

Sonoran Pronghorn: The pronghorn is often mistakenly called the "pronghorn antelope." Actually, the Pronghorn is the only species in its family and is not really an antelope at all. An adult Pronghorn weighs about 100 pounds and stands 3 feet tall at the shoulder. It is tan, with a white rump and two white stripes on its throat. Pronghorns inhabit sage flats and prairies of many western states.

The Sonoran Pronghorn is a kind of Pronghorn that lives only in a few counties of southwestern Arizona. Less than 200 Sonoran Pronghorns remain in the wild. Habitat destruction and hunting have both played a part in this mammal's decline. The life history and habits of the Sonoran Pronghorn are being studied in order to plan its recovery. **(64)**

63. Woodland Caribou

64. Sonoran Pronghorn

39

65. Gray Wolf

Wolves

Gray Wolf: Gray Wolves vary in color from white to black, although most are gray speckled with black. Typical males weigh 100 pounds and are 5 feet long from nose to tail-tip. Wolves were once common in the northern states and throughout Canada. They actually helped the species they hunted by taking the old, weak, and sick animals. But when humans arrived with their herds of cattle and sheep, wolves became a feared nuisance. The U.S. government paid bounties to hunters who killed wolves, and they were hunted, trapped, and poisoned relentlessly.

By the early decades of the 20th century, the Gray Wolf was gone from most of the United States, though it still roams through most of far northern North America. Recently there have been efforts to protect the few remaining U.S. wolves and even to reintroduce families of wolves into their old range in the United States.

Stories about wolves attacking humans are mostly untrue, but wolves will kill livestock. A government program that pays ranchers for lost animals is part of the effort to restore the Gray Wolf to its home. **(65)**

Red Wolf: This southern wolf is smaller than the Gray Wolf. A male Red Wolf usually weighs 70 pounds and measures 4 feet from nose to tip of tail. The Red Wolf used to range through the south-central and southern states. Like its northern cousin, the Red Wolf was hunted and trapped with a vengeance whenever it came in contact with humans. Although it does kill some livestock animals, the Red Wolf preys mainly on rabbits and other rodents that compete for grazing land.

Typical of the hysterical "bad press" that this and other wolves received is this story told by naturalist John Audubon in the mid-19th century: following army battles, said Audubon, "these ravenous beasts disput(ed) the carcasses of the brave, the young, and the patriotic, who have fallen for their country's honour!"

Today, the few Red Wolves that survive eke out an existence in coastal plain scrub of the southeastern states, mainly Texas, Louisiana, and Arkansas. Captive breeding programs have been started to help save the Red Wolf. **(66)**

66. Red Wolf

67. Indiana Bat

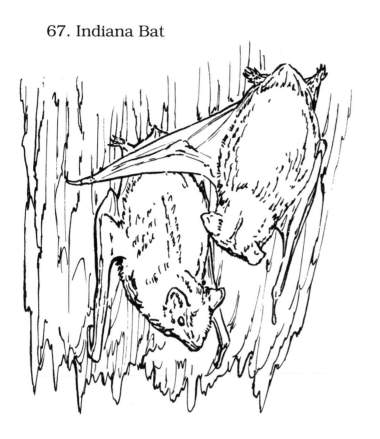

68. Gray Bat

Bats

Bats are another group of mammals that has suffered from "bad press." People once believed that bats would attack people and suck their blood, or get tangled in people's hair. We now know that most kinds of bats are very beneficial because of the enormous number of insects they eat — one of their favorite foods is the mosquito. Some people even put up roosting boxes in their yards for bats to use.

Bats are the only flying mammals. They fly primarily at night, using sonar to find flying insects. Most North American species feed solely on insects; a few species eat pollen and nectar. Bats spend the day hanging upside down in their roosts in trees, caves, barns, or other quiet spots.

In summer, females of some species gather in common roosts to rear their babies together. Newborns will cling to their mothers as they fly.

Some kinds of bats spend the winter hibernating in caves, while others migrate to warmer places.

Indiana Bat: The diminutive (just 2 inches) Indiana Bat is gray-brown on top and cinnamon below. This species used to range over much of the eastern and midwestern United States.

Today, most populations winter in Indiana, Kentucky, and Missouri. People who count these large populations noted that in the early 1980s, their numbers declined by half. Bats often die because humans disturb them when they are hibernating, so conservationists are trying to keep people out of bat caves. **(67)**

Gray Bat: The Gray Bat is reddish brown. This southeastern bat hibernates in large colonies in limestone caves. Like the Indiana Bat, the Gray Bat is most threatened by humans entering their winter caves. Hibernating bats have only enough fat reserves to carry them through the winter, so death rates are high in colonies where the bats must use up energy escaping from intruders. **(68)**

Sanborn's Longnose Bat and **Mexican Longnose Bat:** These two bats live mainly in Mexico. They are unusual in North America because they feed on the pollen and nectar of cactus and century plants. The bats and their food plants are dependent on each other, as bats are the major pollinators of the plants.

Outside of Mexico, Sanborn's Longnose Bat **(69)** occurs mainly in Arizona, and the Mexican Longnose Bat **(70)** has been reported only at a single site in Big Bend National Park in western Texas. Both species have declined because of human disturbance and the destruction of their food plants.

69. Sanborn's Longnose Bat

70. Mexican Longnose Bat

43

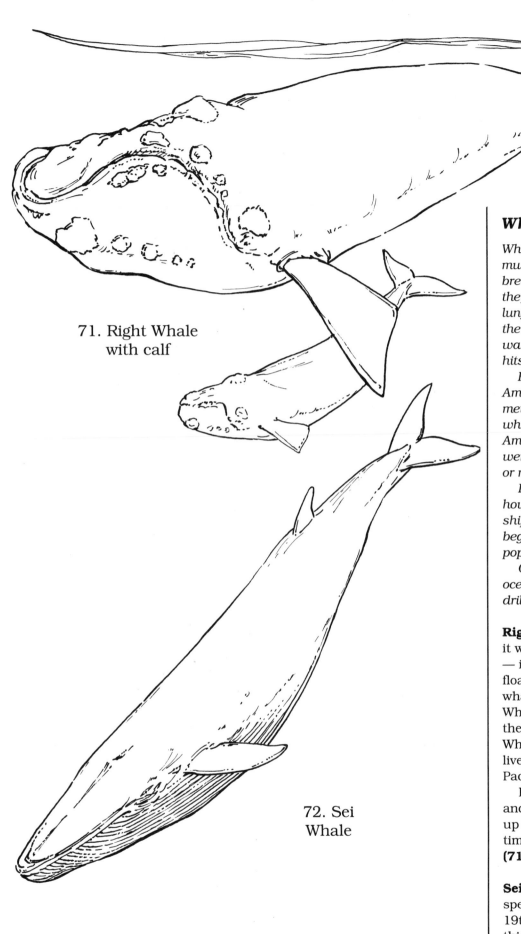

71. Right Whale
with calf

72. Sei
Whale

Whales

Whales are marine mammals that must come to the surface to breathe. Just before they surface, they spout the air from their lungs. Often one can see vapor in the seawater spray; this is their warm breath condensing when it hits the cool air.

For thousands of years, native Americans, using traditional methods and tools, hunted whales along the coasts of North America. Because their methods were primitive, hunting had little or no effect on whale populations.

During the 19th century, however, commercial whaling ships in all of the world's oceans began to seriously deplete whale populations.

Other threats to the whales are ocean pollution, ocean oil-well drilling, and human disturbances.

Right Whale: So named because it was the "right" one for hunting — it was easy to catch and floated when killed. Commercial whalers slaughtered Right Whales by the thousands. Now there may be less than 750 Right Whales left in the world. They live in both the Atlantic and Pacific oceans.

Right Whales are blackish, and grow to 70 feet. They spout up to 15 feet in the air, sometimes in two sprays forming a V. **(71)**

Sei Whale: This whale was speedy enough to escape the 19th-century whaling ships. In this century, though, deisel-powered whaling fleets armed with sophisticated tracking devices and harpoons with

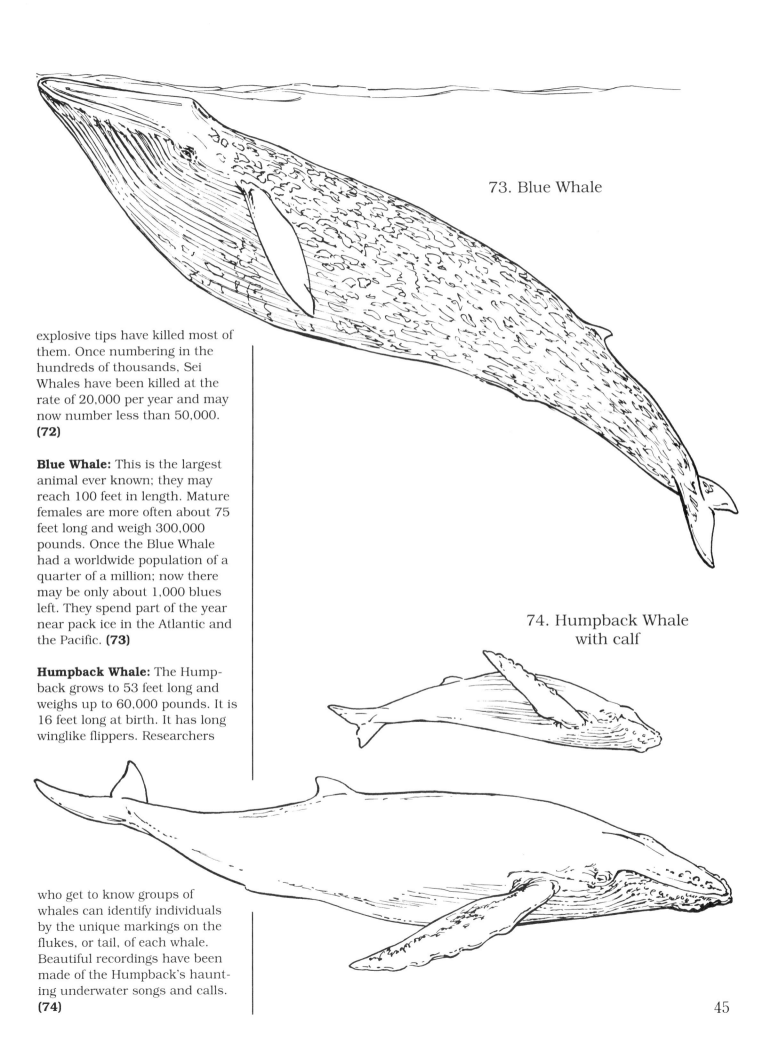

73. Blue Whale

explosive tips have killed most of them. Once numbering in the hundreds of thousands, Sei Whales have been killed at the rate of 20,000 per year and may now number less than 50,000. **(72)**

Blue Whale: This is the largest animal ever known; they may reach 100 feet in length. Mature females are more often about 75 feet long and weigh 300,000 pounds. Once the Blue Whale had a worldwide population of a quarter of a million; now there may be only about 1,000 blues left. They spend part of the year near pack ice in the Atlantic and the Pacific. **(73)**

Humpback Whale: The Humpback grows to 53 feet long and weighs up to 60,000 pounds. It is 16 feet long at birth. It has long winglike flippers. Researchers

74. Humpback Whale
with calf

who get to know groups of whales can identify individuals by the unique markings on the flukes, or tail, of each whale. Beautiful recordings have been made of the Humpback's haunting underwater songs and calls. **(74)**

45

Wild Cats

Ocelot: Adult male ocelots are 4 feet long and weigh up to 25 pounds; females are a little smaller. Their handsome tawny coat is heavily marked with black spots and stripes. Ocelots prefer the thickets of subtropical forests, but a few live in extreme southern Texas and perhaps Arizona.

The pressure to clear land for agriculture and housing in southern Texas has drastically reduced the Ocelot's habitat of brush and floodplain forest along the Rio Grande.

In the 19th century, hunters used Ocelot pelts to make bullet pouches. Today, this cat is still killed for its beautiful fur. **(75)**

Lynx: The Lynx, a medium-sized cat, prefers far northern forests and is uncommon in the U.S. It is similar to the more southerly Bobcat but has longer legs and very large feet, which help it walk over the snow. It hunts mostly Snowshoe Hares. The Lynx can grow to 3½ feet and weigh as much as 40 pounds. Its fur color ranges from gray to tawny and is sparsely marked with dark streaks and spots below.

Late in the 19th century, as many as 80,000 of these cats were trapped by North American fur traders in one year. Lynx pelts are still highly valued and bring between $650 and $1000. **(76)**

75. Ocelot

76. Lynx

46

Squirrels

Mount Graham Red Squirrel: This small form of the common Red Squirrel occurs only in the Pinaleno Mountains of southeastern Arizona. The threat to its habitat comes from an unlikely source: astronomy. The University of Arizona plans to build several astronomy observatories in the Pinalenos Mountains, including one on Mount Graham. The mountains are good places for observing the stars because they are far away from the lights of the cities. But the Mount Graham Red Squirrel is protected by the Endangered Species Act, and some conservationists fear that new roads and buildings in its habitat could reduce its numbers. This little squirrel has been the cause of several court battles, and its fate is still undecided. **(77)**

Delmarva Peninsula Fox Squirrel: This is a form of the Eastern Fox Squirrel, which can be found in many hardwood and pine forests east of the Rockies except in New England and New York. These squirrels are generally larger than the common Eastern Gray Squirrel, and there are yellow, gray, and reddish color forms.

The Delmarva Peninsula Fox Squirrel typically occurs in loblolly pine forests on the peninsula of Maryland and Virginia. Because many of the original forests have been cut to make way for farms and urban development, fox squirrels are being squeezed into smaller and smaller areas. **(78)**

77. Mount Graham
Red Squirrel

78. Delmarva
Peninsula
Fox Squirrel

47

79. Swift Fox

80. Utah
Prairie Dog

Swift Fox: This small, tawny and gray fox has large ears and a long, bushy, black-tipped tail. Originally an inhabitant of the central plains from Texas to Canada, this northern race of the Kit Fox has disappeared from Canada and presently lives in small numbers in Montana and the Dakotas. While agricultural land use has taken much of the foxes' original habitat, poison bait meant for wolves and coyotes has also killed many Swift Foxes. **(79)**

Utah Prairie Dog: Early explorers described with amazement how prairie dogs formed large colonies called "towns." One prairie dog town in Texas was said to be 250 miles long and 150 miles wide.

Unfortunately for the prairie dogs, they competed for pasture with grazing animals. Farmers and ranchers who settled the plains poisoned prairie dogs in huge numbers. Between the 1920s and the 1970s, two-thirds of all Utah Prairie Dogs were killed. Fortunately, they are now protected, and the species has begun to recover. **(80)**

Kangaroo rats are named for their long hind legs, feet, and tail. They all have cheek pouches for carrying seeds. Although kangaroo rats occur in several western states, California has the distinction of having six endangered species of kangaroo rats.

Giant Kangaroo Rat: A giant only to other kangaroo rats, this 6-inch animal has an 8-inch tail. It is brown on top with a white belly. Much of its dry grassland habitat has been plowed under for agricultural use. **(81)**

Stephen's Kangaroo Rat: This species is only a little smaller than the Giant Kangaroo Rat. Its dark brown coat is speckled with gray. Several of the remaining groups of Stephen's Kangaroo Rats live on privately owned land. Because this animal is listed under the Endangered Species Act, some land owners are worried that the kangaroo rat will hurt the value of the land if the owners are not allowed to develop it. **(82)**

Fresno Kangaroo Rat: A buff-colored animal, just ten inches from the tip of the nose to the tip of the tail. It lives only in one place in California, a habitat that once included about 250,000 acres. Unfortunately, all but about 1% of that site has been developed for agriculture or housing. **(83)**

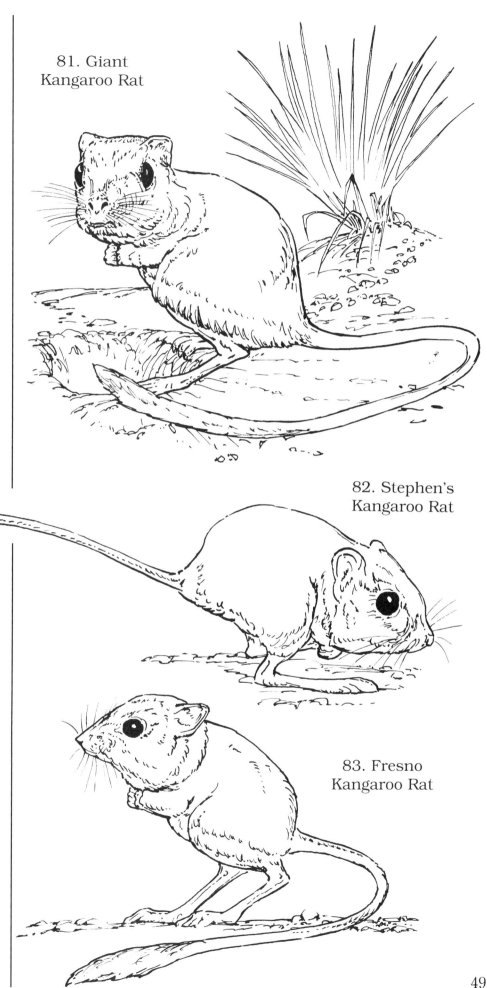

81. Giant Kangaroo Rat

82. Stephen's Kangaroo Rat

83. Fresno Kangaroo Rat

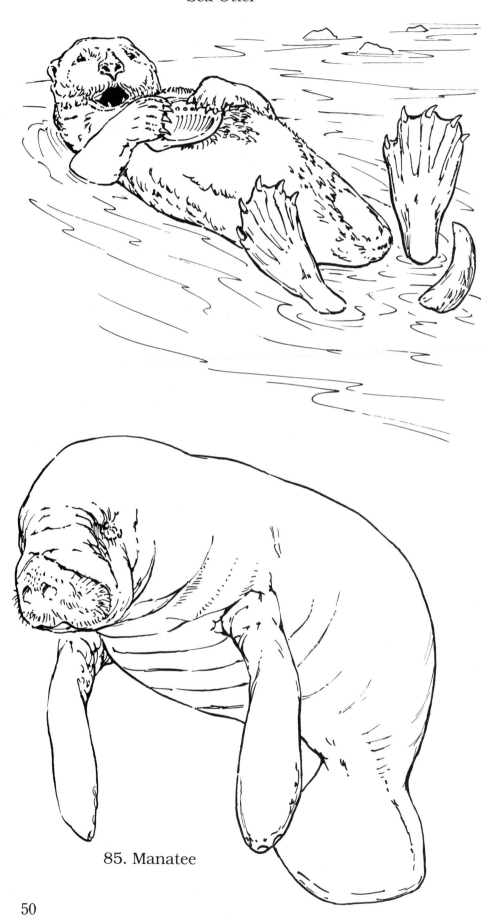

84. Southern
Sea Otter

85. Manatee

Southern Sea Otter: Three feet long and weighing up to 85 pounds, the sea otter has glossy black or dark brown fur tipped with white. The sea otter's head and neck are yellowish, and its toes are webbed. This species swims and feeds near seaweed beds close to shore, where it dives for shellfish. After it catches a meal, the otter floats on its back, using its chest as a dinner plate. When the otter takes a nap, it wraps itself up in the long strands of seaweed so it won't float away while it sleeps.

In the 19th century, pelt hunters almost spelled an end to the Sea Otter. Today, shell fisheries view the otters as unwanted competitors. Fortunately, otters are now protected, and their colonies on the West Coast are growing. **(84)**

Manatee: This large mammal spends its whole life in the water. Though it looks a little like a whale, it is not related to whales or porpoises. The Manatee grows to 13 feet long and may weigh over a ton. It has front flippers like a seal, but no hind flippers. Manatees, or sea cows, are slow animals that spend much of their time basking near the surface and grazing on aquatic plants in warm coastal rivers and marshes. In the waters around Florida, this puts Manatees right in the path of a large number of motor boats. Because they are sluggish and stay near the surface, the Manatee is nearly always the loser in such an encounter. Most Manatees seen in Florida waters have wounds and scars caused by the propellers of power boats, and deaths from such clashes are rising. **(85)**

Endangered Fishes

Darters

Darters are small fish that live in freshwater streams and lakes. They "dart" about on the bottom, eating small insects. There are more than 100 species of darters, and each one is worthy of our protection.

Snail Darter: This tiny fish is probably the most famous threatened fish in North America. The Snail Darter, 3½ inches long, is tannish yellow with several dark brown bars across the back. It was the cause of a dispute over a project to build a dam on the Little Tennessee River, called the Tellico Dam. The Little Tennessee River was home to the only known population of Snail Darters. Because the Snail Darter is protected by the Endangered Species Act, there was a series of legal battles, and the dam project was finally stopped. The Snail Darter has now been introduced to other locations. **(86)**

Watercress Darter: This colorful, 2-inch darter has numerous dark spots on top and a red belly. The dorsal fins are striped with red and blue. The Watercress Darter lives only in a few springs in Jefferson County, Alabama. Pollution and urban development have damaged the springs and endangered this species. **(87)**

Maryland Darter: The Maryland Darter is about 3 inches long. It is silvery with dark bars across the back and dark markings around the eye. Its only known habitat, the Susquehanna River, has been badly polluted and radically changed by dams. **(88)**

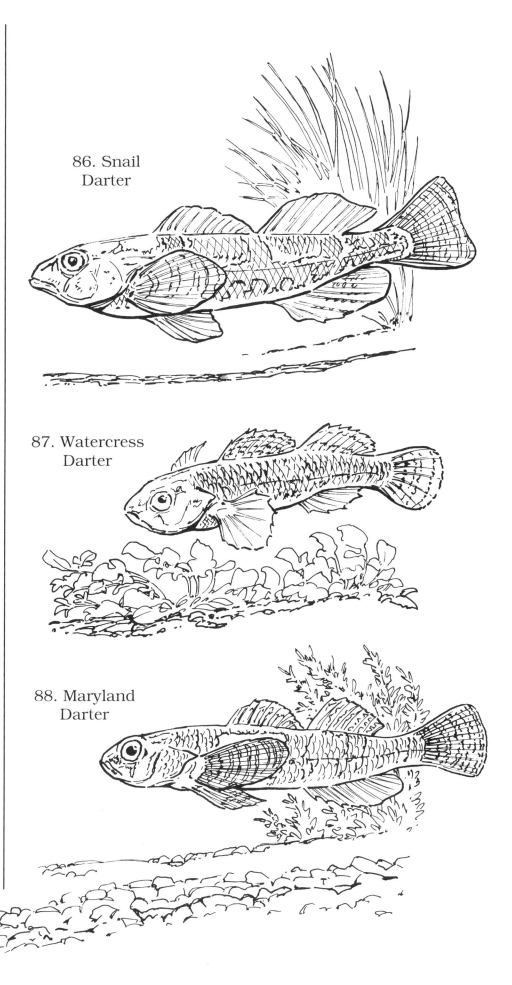

86. Snail Darter

87. Watercress Darter

88. Maryland Darter

89. Shortnose Sturgeon

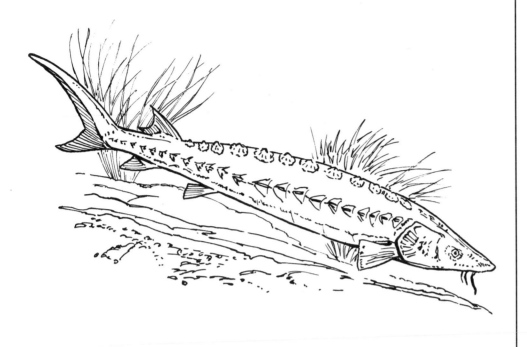

90. Striped Bass

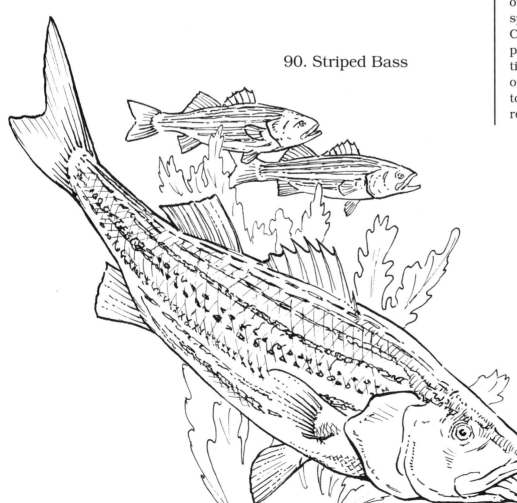

Fishes

Shortnose Sturgeon: This rather strange-looking fish has a long snout and rows of shields down its back and along its sides. The Shortnose Sturgeon is black with olive hues on top; its lower sides are reddish violet and its belly is white. Once common in the rivers that run into the Atlantic, this sturgeon has all but disappeared. **(89)**

Striped Bass: The North Atlantic Striped Bass was the subject of the first conservation law passed in North America in 1639. It has always been an important sport and food fish. The Striped Bass is olive green on top and silvery below. The stripes on its sides give the fish its name. Mature fish often weigh over 50 pounds.

In the early 1970s an alarming crash in the Striped Bass population was noted. Acid rain and other water pollution in the fish's spawning areas, such as the Chesapeake Bay, may have all played a part. Recent conservation efforts and a temporary halt on catching Striped Bass seems to have helped this species recover. **(90)**

Cui-ui: The Cui-ui (pronounced *kwee wee*) is a large fish that belongs to a group called suckers. Suckers have small mouths and large lips, with which they "vacuum" up their food from the bottoms of streams and lakes. The Cui-ui lives only in Pyramid Lake, Nevada, spawning every spring in the Truckee River. Much of the water in the Truckee has been claimed for farming and household use. This has drastically lowered the birth rates of the Cui-ui. By the 1960s the Cui-ui was endangered. **(91)**

Paiute Trout: The Paiute Trout is one of several endangered forms of the Cutthroat Trout, so called because of the red mark under its lower jaw. Paiute Trout occur in only a few mountain streams in California. Because their home territory is small, Paiutes have never been very numerous, and there may now be only about 2,000 of them.

A major threat to the Paiute Trout has been hybridization with other, non-native, trout species introduced by state Fish and Game workers. Efforts are underway to protect the Paiutes' habitat from livestock and from accidental introduction of other trout species. **(92)**

91. Cui-ui

92. Paiute Trout

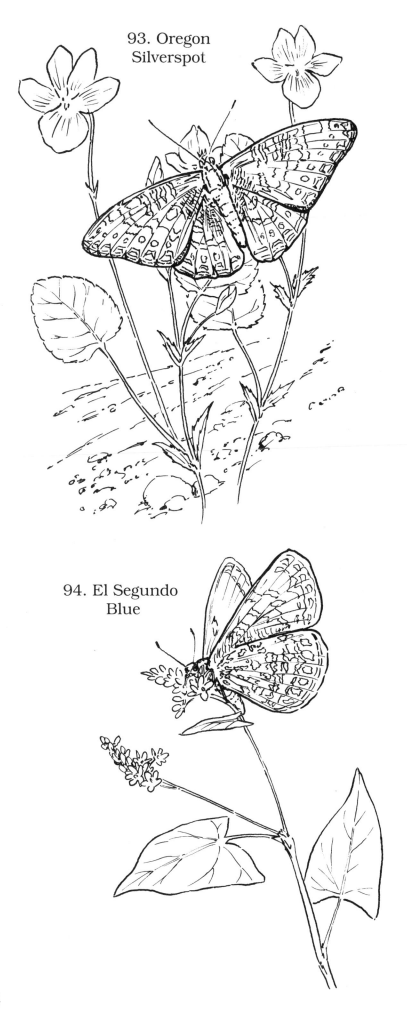

93. Oregon
Silverspot

94. El Segundo
Blue

Endangered Insects

Butterflies

Butterflies depend on their host plants for survival, so they are quickly affected by damage to their habitats. A few species are also endangered by collectors.

Oregon Silverspot: This butterfly lives along the coast of Oregon. It is a dark form of a butterfly called the Zerene Fritillary. While Zerene Fritillaries are common in some places, many of the coastal meadows and foothills where they live are being developed. When the stands of violets upon which the Oregon Silverspots depend are destroyed, the butterflies disappear. They are rusty orange on top with black markings, and reddish brown below. **(93)**

El Segundo Blue: The El Segundo Blue is one of eight forms of the Square-spotted Blue butterfly living in California. El Segundo Blues depend on the buckwheat plant, which is found in sand dunes near Los Angeles and San Diego. As more and more beachfront properties are developed, there are fewer dunes and fewer El Segundo Blues. They are violet blue on top with a narrow black border; underneath they are silvery gray with black spots and a red band on the hindwing. **(94)**

Lange's Metalmark: Lange's Metalmark is an endangered race of the Mormon Metalmark that occurs in small numbers in Antioch, California. This striking brick red and black butterfly lives in coastal dunes, where several endangered plants also teeter on the brink of extinction. **(95)**

Regal Fritillary: Once widespread from the northern Great Plains eastward, the Regal Fritillary has disappeared from much of its former range, particularly in the East. A grasslands species, this butterfly occurs in mountain pastures, tall-grass prairies, and wet meadows. The Regal Fritillary's numbers have dropped steeply, probably because many of its grassland habitats have been destroyed. On its upper side, it has orange forewings with dark borders and dark hindwings. Below, it has white V-shaped markings on its forewings and large silver spots on its hindwings. **(96)**

95. Lange's Metalmark

96. Regal Fritillary

Beetles

If sheer diversity and numbers are the yardstick, we might well describe Earth as the planet of the beetles. One estimate is that three out of every four animals are beetles. Most likely there are tens of thousands of beetle species that have not yet been discovered. No one knows how many of these insects are endangered or threatened. Even when species are known to be in danger, most people are less sympathetic to the problems of beetles than they are to those of more "cuddly" animals such as mammals.

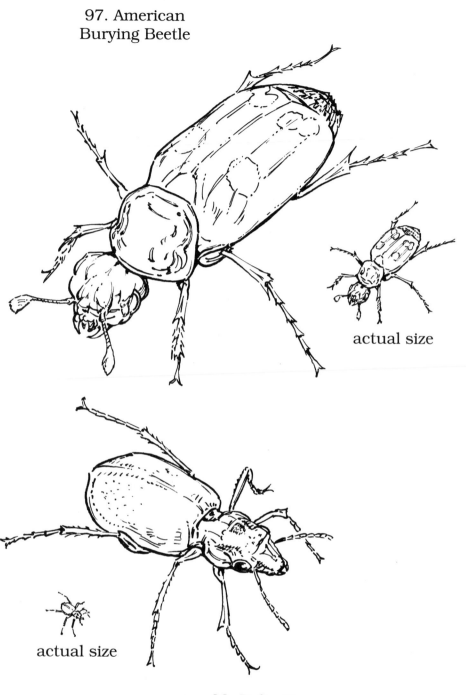

97. American Burying Beetle

actual size

actual size

98. Delta Green Ground Beetle

American Burying Beetle: Burying beetles are also known as carrion beetles because they search for and bury the remains of small mammals, birds, and reptiles. The grave then becomes a nest stocked with food for the next generation of beetles. This large (over 1 inch) beetle is black with red markings.

The American Burying Beetle was once common throughout much of the eastern United States. It is now found only in two sites, one in eastern Oklahoma and the other on Block Island, Rhode Island. The reason for its near disappearance is not known, but efforts are being made to save this beetle, including reintroduction programs. **(97)**

Delta Green Ground Beetle: This small (¼ inch) ground beetle is bronze on top and metallic green below. It lives in central California, in pools that are usually wet only in the spring. Many kinds of frogs, salamanders, and insects also depend on these pools to provide a mating area and a nursery for the next generation. Humans have used much of the water in this area, lowering the water table and causing many of these pools to dry up. **(98)**

Valley Elderberry Longhorn Beetle: This large (2 inches) beetle is metallic green on top with a reddish orange border. It is named for its favorite food, elderberry. Its natural habitat in central California is disappearing, but a sizable piece of land along the American River Parkway in Sacramento County has been set aside as a refuge for the Valley Elderberry Longhorn Beetle. **(99)**

Northeastern Beach Tiger Beetle: This brownish green tiger beetle with large cream-colored markings on its wing covers once occurred in great swarms. It is now nearly extinct, and lives only in a few small colonies between Cape Cod and the central New Jersey coast. Because the larvae burrow in the sand just above the high tide mark, many are killed by off-road vehicles and pedestrian traffic. **(100)**

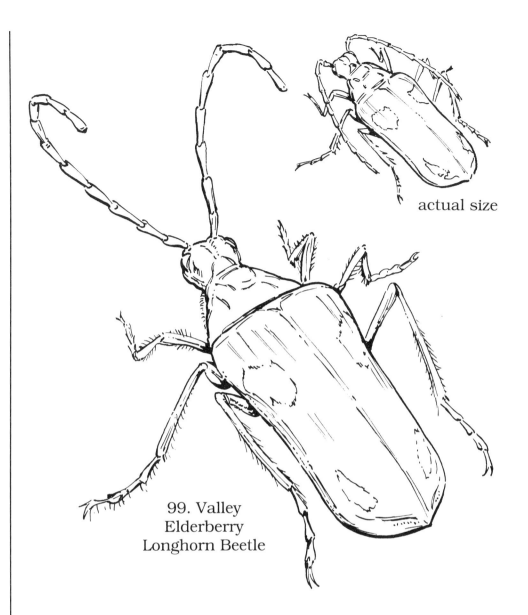

actual size

99. Valley Elderberry Longhorn Beetle

100. Northeastern Beach Tiger Beetle

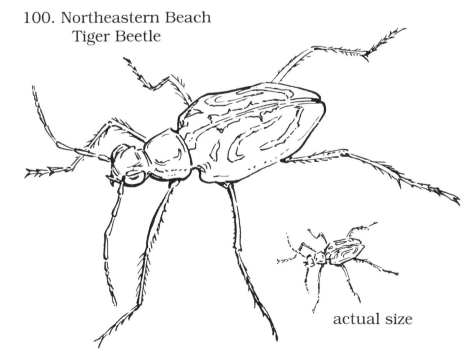

actual size

101. Painted Snake Coiled
Forest Snail

102. Noonday Snail

Land Snails

Although land snails are often overlooked, even by naturalists, they are common in North America. More than 750 species have been described in the continental United States. Many of our native snails are solitary, meaning they live alone or in small groups, unlike other snail species that live in colonies and are pests on crops. Many kinds of land snails have both male and female sexual organs.

The endangered and threatened land snails shown here all have relatively small ranges. Each population is also relatively small. Some species have only a few hundred individuals. Because they have small ranges and populations, these land snails can be wiped out by natural or man-made pressures that would not affect more numerous and widespread animals. Just one new housing development, or pesticides applied to one farm, could cause the extinction of some of these species.

Painted Snake Coiled Forest Snail: About 1 inch long and ½ inch wide, this snail is off-white, with many brown blotches and whorls. Found in Buck Creek Cove in southern Tennessee. **(101)**

Noonday Snail: This species is glossy red and less than an inch long. The Noonday Snail occurs in the Nantahala Gorge in western North Carolina. **(102)**

Magazine Mountain Shagreen: This snail is about half an inch long and is colored light brown. It is found only in the Ozark National Forest in Logan County, Arkansas. **(103)**

Stock Island Snail: This large tree snail is over 2 inches long; it is buff-colored with purple bands. It lives in Monroe County, Florida, on several of the keys. **(104)**

Virginia Fringed Mountain Snail: This tiny land snail measures less than two tenths of an inch across. It is mostly pale greenish brown and lives on the New River in Pulaski County, Virginia. **(105)**

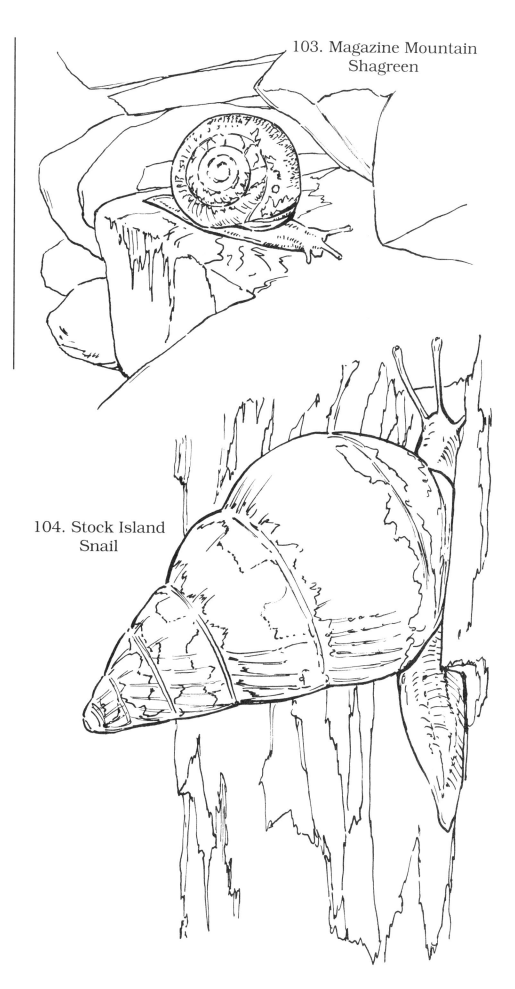

103. Magazine Mountain Shagreen

104. Stock Island Snail

actual size

105. Virginia Fringed Mountain Snail

59

106. American
Crocodile

107. Bald Eagle

Success Stories

American Crocodile: Much less common and with a smaller range than the American Alligator, the American Crocodile lives only in southern Florida, usually in brackish water. This impressive reptile may grow to 12 feet long and feeds mainly on fish. The crocodile's habitat been severely reduced, and it has also suffered from overhunting. Crocodile-skin shoes, hat bands, and belts have always been popular. By the 1970s, there were only a few dozen crocodiles left in Florida. At that low point, a law was passed against hunting crocodiles, and the Crocodile Lake National Wildlife Refuge was established. Now there are more than 500 American Crocodiles living in the wild. **(106)**

Bald Eagle: For decades, Bald Eagles have been hunted and poisoned, and their habitat destroyed. In the 1940s, DDT pesticides also took a heavy toll on the Bald Eagle. In the 1960s and early 1970s, the eagle's numbers were still dropping.

Fortunately, DDT was banned, and programs were started to help bring back the Bald Eagle. Now, healthy populations of the bird that is our national symbol can be found from the Chesapeake Bay to the state of Washington. **(107)**

Peregrine Falcon: A magnificent bird of prey, the peregrine lives all over the world. But the race that occupied the eastern United States was virtually wiped out by DDT. The ban against such chemicals in the early 1970s made it possible to bring back our peregrines. Methods for doing this have included breeding the birds in captivity, bringing in eggs from threatened nests, and releasing the falcons back into the wild. In some places, peregrines have adapted to city life. They nest high on skyscrapers and bridges and hunt pigeons and starlings. Peregrine Falcons are still protected by law across the country. **(108)**

108. Peregrine Falcon

61

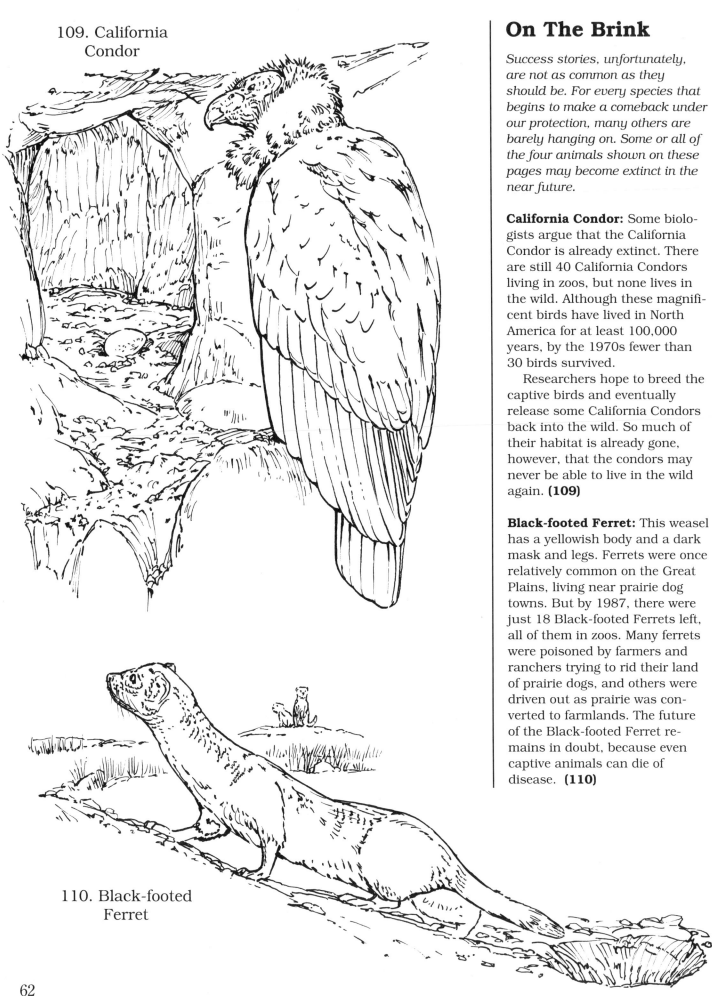

109. California Condor

On The Brink

Success stories, unfortunately, are not as common as they should be. For every species that begins to make a comeback under our protection, many others are barely hanging on. Some or all of the four animals shown on these pages may become extinct in the near future.

California Condor: Some biologists argue that the California Condor is already extinct. There are still 40 California Condors living in zoos, but none lives in the wild. Although these magnificent birds have lived in North America for at least 100,000 years, by the 1970s fewer than 30 birds survived.

Researchers hope to breed the captive birds and eventually release some California Condors back into the wild. So much of their habitat is already gone, however, that the condors may never be able to live in the wild again. **(109)**

Black-footed Ferret: This weasel has a yellowish body and a dark mask and legs. Ferrets were once relatively common on the Great Plains, living near prairie dog towns. But by 1987, there were just 18 Black-footed Ferrets left, all of them in zoos. Many ferrets were poisoned by farmers and ranchers trying to rid their land of prairie dogs, and others were driven out as prairie was converted to farmlands. The future of the Black-footed Ferret remains in doubt, because even captive animals can die of disease. **(110)**

110. Black-footed Ferret

Eskimo Curlew: During the 1970s many ornithologists were convinced the Eskimo Curlew was extinct. A handful of bird watchers, however, claimed that they had seen the curlew and that small groups of the birds still existed. In 1987 a small breeding population of Eskimo Curlews was reported in northern Canada. Because little is known about the life cycle and habits of this species, it is hard to plan how to help the Eskimo Curlew recover. **(111)**

Ivory-billed Woodpecker: These woodpeckers used to live in cypress swamps and dense forests along river banks in the southeastern states. During the late 1980s Jerome Jackson, an expert on North American woodpeckers, searched that area in a last-ditch attempt to find an Ivory-billed Woodpecker. Although there were tantalizing reports and plenty of rumors, Jackson found no Ivory-billeds.

This large (20 inches, not including tail) black and white species, the male with a red crest, was fairly common in the 19th century. By the beginning of the 20th century, however, logging and hunting had severely reduced its numbers. The last confirmed sighting of an Ivory-billed Woodpecker occurred in the 1940s. In all probability the Ivory-billed Woodpecker is gone forever. **(112)**

111. Eskimo Curlew

112. Ivory-billed Woodpecker

63

Index

Akiapolaau, 19
Auk, Great, 11

Bass, Striped, 52
Bat, Gray, 42
   Hawaiian Hoary, 18
   Indiana, 42
   Mexican Longnose, 43
   Sanborn's Longnose, 43
Bear, Grizzly, 38
   Short-faced, 8
Beetle, American Burying, 56
   Delta Green Ground, 57
   Northeastern Beach Tiger, 57
   Valley Elderberry Longhorn, 57
Blue, El Segundo, 54
   Xerces, 10
Boa, Puerto Rican, 31
Butterflies, 54–55

Caracara, Audubon's Crested, 22
Caribou, Woodland, 39
Clapper Rail, Light-footed, 29
Condor, California, 62
   Merriam's Giant, 8
Coral, Boulder, 16
   Brain, 16
   Sea Fan, 16
Crane, Mississippi Sandhill, 28
   Whooping, 28
Crocodile, American, 60
Curlew, Eskimo, 63
Cui-ui, 53

Darter, Snail, 51
   Maryland, 51
   Watercress, 51

Eagle, Bald, 60
Eastern Indigo Snake, 15
Elkhorn Coral, 16
Endangered Species Act, 4

Falcon, Peregrine, 61
Ferret, Black-footed, 62
Fisher, 13
Fox, Swift, 48
Fritillary, Regal, 55

Goose, Hawaiian, *see* Nene

Harvestman, Bee Creek Cave, 30
Hawaiian Hoary Bat, 18
Hawksbill, 35

Kangaroo Rat, Fresno, 49
   Giant, 49
   Stephen's, 49
Kite, Snail, 20

Least Tern, 24
Leatherback, 35
Lizard, Coachella Valley Fringe-toed, 33
Loggerhead, 34
Lynx, 46

Manatee, 50
Mastodon, American, 9
Metalmark, Lange's, 55
Murrelet, Marbled, 13

Nene, 19

Ocelot, 46
Otter, Southern Sea, 50
Owl, Spotted, 12

Panther, Florida, 21
Pelican, Brown, 23
Pigeon, Passenger, 11
Plover, Piping, 24
Prairie Chicken, Attwater's, 29
Prairie Dog, Utah, 48
Pronghorn, Sonoran, 39
Pseudoscorpion, Tooth Cave, 30

Rattlesnake, New Mexico Ridgenose, 31
Ridley, 35

Salamander, Santa Cruz Long-toed, 36
   Texas Blind, 36
Sea Cow, Stellar's, 10
Sea Fan, 16
Silverspot, Oregon, 54
Snail, Magazine Mountain Shagreen, 59

Noonday, 58
Painted Snake Coiled Forest, 58
Stock Island, 59
Virginia Fringed Mountain, 59
Snails, Oahu tree, 18
Snake, Atlantic Salt Marsh, 31
   Eastern Indigo, 15
   San Francisco Garter, 32
Spider, Tooth Cave, 30
Squirrel, Delmarva Peninsula Red, 47
   Mount Graham Red, 47
Stork, Wood, 22
Sturgeon, Shortnose, 52
Swallowtail, Schaus', 20

Tern, Least, 24
   Roseate, 25
Toad, Houston, 37
   Wyoming, 37
Tortoise, Desert, 32
   Gopher, 15
Triceratops, 6
Trout, Paiute, 53
Turtle, Green, 34
   Plymouth Redbelly, 33
Tyrannosaurus rex, 6

Vireo, Black-capped, 26

Warbler, Bachman's, 27
   Golden-cheeker, 26
   Kirtland's, 27
Whale, Blue, 45
   Humpback, 45
   Right, 44
   Sei, 44
Wolf, Dire, 9
   Gray, 40
   Red, 41
Woodpecker, Ivory-billed, 63
   Red-cockaded, 14

48

50

52

54

49

51

53

55

56

57

59

61

63

62

64

58

60

67

69

65

66

68

70